What Has **Wide, Padded Feet** and Spits?

WRITTEN BY **Robert Kanner**

ILLUSTRATED BY **Russ Daff**

·... dingles & company New Jersey

FOR MARTY GATTI

First Printing

Published by dingles&company
P.O. Box 508
Sea Girt, New Jersey 08750

**LIBRARY OF CONGRESS
CATALOG CARD NUMBER**
2007903693

ISBN
978-1-59646-784-2

Printed in the United States
of America

The Uncover & Discover series is
based on the original concept
of Judy Mazzeo Zocchi.

ART DIRECTION & DESIGN
Rizco Design

EDITORIAL CONSULTANT
Andrea Curley

PROJECT MANAGER
Lisa Aldorasi

EDUCATIONAL CONSULTANTS
Melissa Oster and Margaret Bergin

CREATIVE DIRECTOR
Barbie Lambert

PRE-PRESS
Pixel Graphics

WEBSITE
www.dingles.com

E-MAIL
info@dingles.com

The **Uncover & Discover** series encourages children to inquire, investigate, and use their imagination in an interactive and entertaining manner. This series helps to sharpen their powers of observation, improve reading and writing skills, and apply knowledge across the curriculum.

Uncover each one and see you can when you're

clue one by
what mammal
disco**ver**
done!

My **ears** are small and are lined with thick hair to keep out sand and dust.

WHERE IS THE **EAR?**

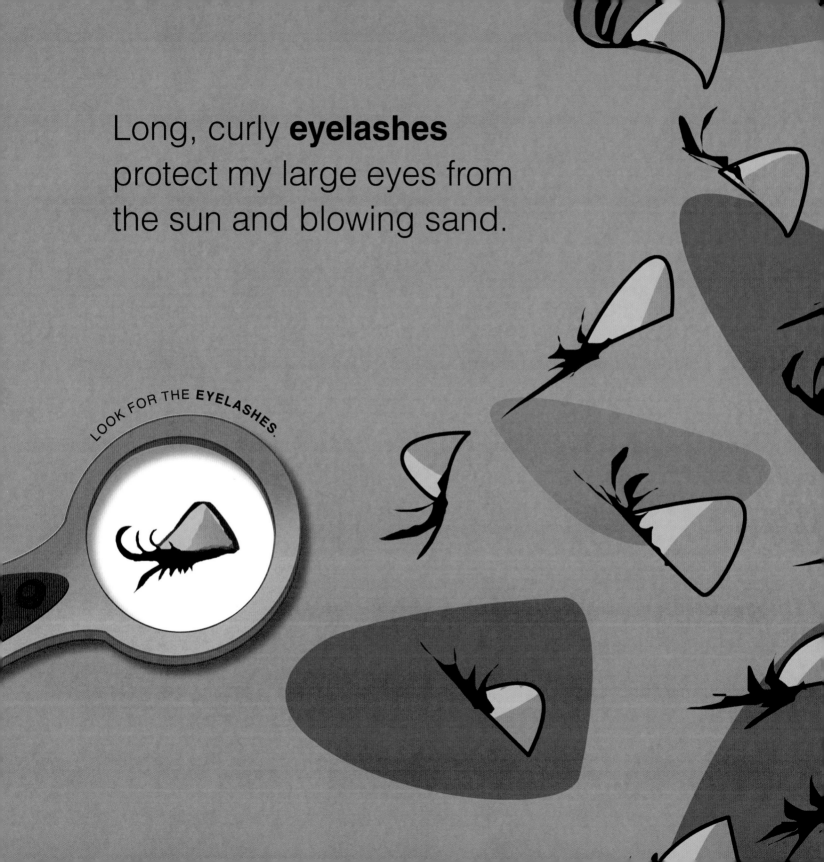

Long, curly **eyelashes** protect my large eyes from the sun and blowing sand.

LOOK FOR THE **EYELASHES**.

Bushy, overhanging **eyebrows** shield my eyes from the hot sun.

FIND THE **EYEBROW**.

My large, slitlike **nostrils** can close completely to keep out sand.

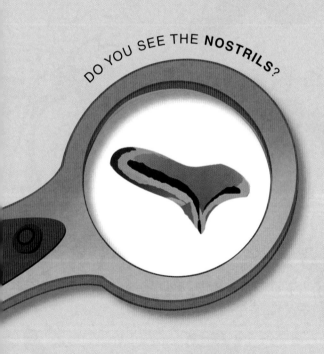

DO YOU SEE THE **NOSTRILS**?

My thick **lips** have tough, stiff hairs on them. These hairs allow me to pull thorny desert plants into my mouth without feeling any pain.

WHERE ARE THE **LIPS?**

To stand up after resting, I lean my **chest** against the ground for support. Its thick, leathery patch of skin protects me from the heat of the hot sand.

LOOK FOR THE **CHEST**.

The **fleshy mound** on my back stores fat, which I use for energy when food is hard to find.

FIND THE **FLESHY MOUND**.

I have long, slender **legs** with strong muscles that allow me to carry heavy loads over long distances.

DO YOU SEE THE **LEG?**

I have thick, tough, bare skin pads on my **knees** that protect them when I kneel in the hot sand.

WHERE IS THE **KNEE?**

I have two **toes**
on each foot.

LOOK FOR THE **TOES**.

Flat, leathery **pads** connect
my toes. When I walk, the pads
spread apart and prevent me
from sinking into the sand.

FIND THE **PAD**.

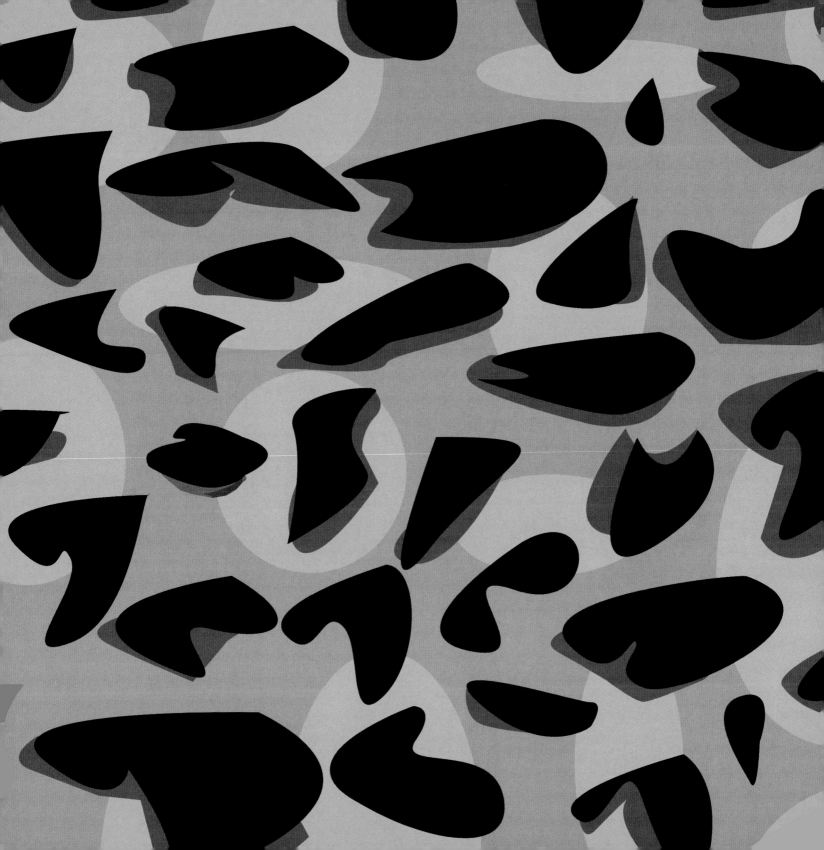

My ropelike **tail** is about 19 inches long, which is very short for my size.

DO YOU SEE THE **TAIL**?

You have uncovered the clues. **Have you guessed what I am?**

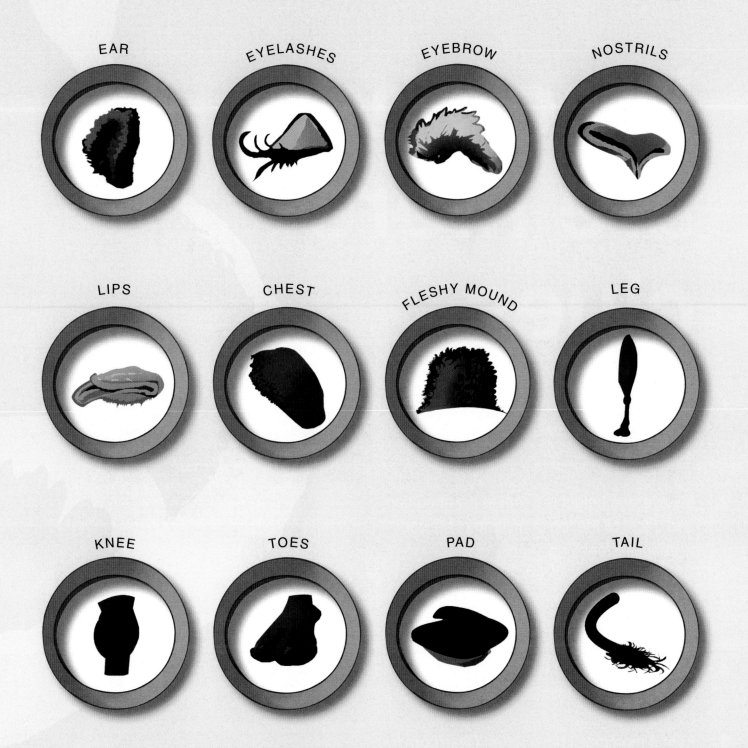

EAR   EYELASHES   EYEBROW   NOSTRILS

LIPS   CHEST   FLESHY MOUND   LEG

KNEE   TOES   PAD   TAIL

If not, here are more clues.

1. I can go for a week or more without drinking water and can survive for several months without food.

2. My average height is 6 feet to my shoulder and 7 feet to the top of my hump. My body is about 10 feet long.

3. I can weigh between 1,000 and 1,500 pounds, about the same weight as a dairy cow.

4. I live in the desert. My relatives can be found in North Africa, the Middle East, and Australia.

5. I am a mammal. I have fur and was born live.

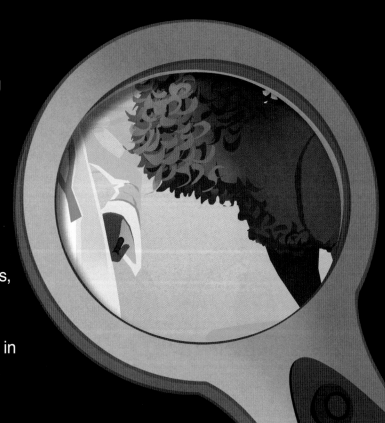

6. I am an only child—my mother has only one calf at a time. She nursed me for one year.

7. I am a herbivore, which means I am a plant eater. I digest food in two steps. After I eat my food I regurgitate this half-digested form, called cud, into my mouth. Then I eat the cud.

8. If I am surprised or feel threatened, I can spit out my cud. The bad smell of it will stay on whomever it hits for days!

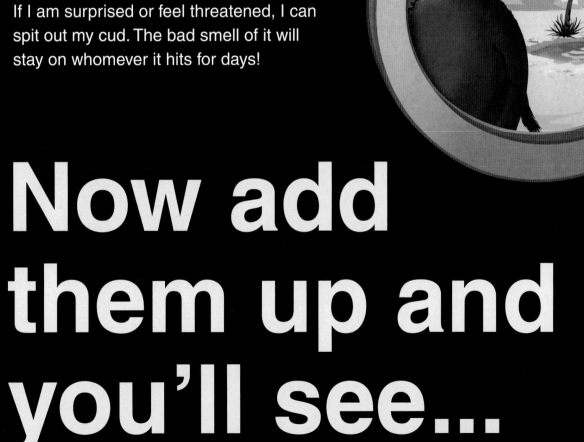

Now add them up and you'll see...

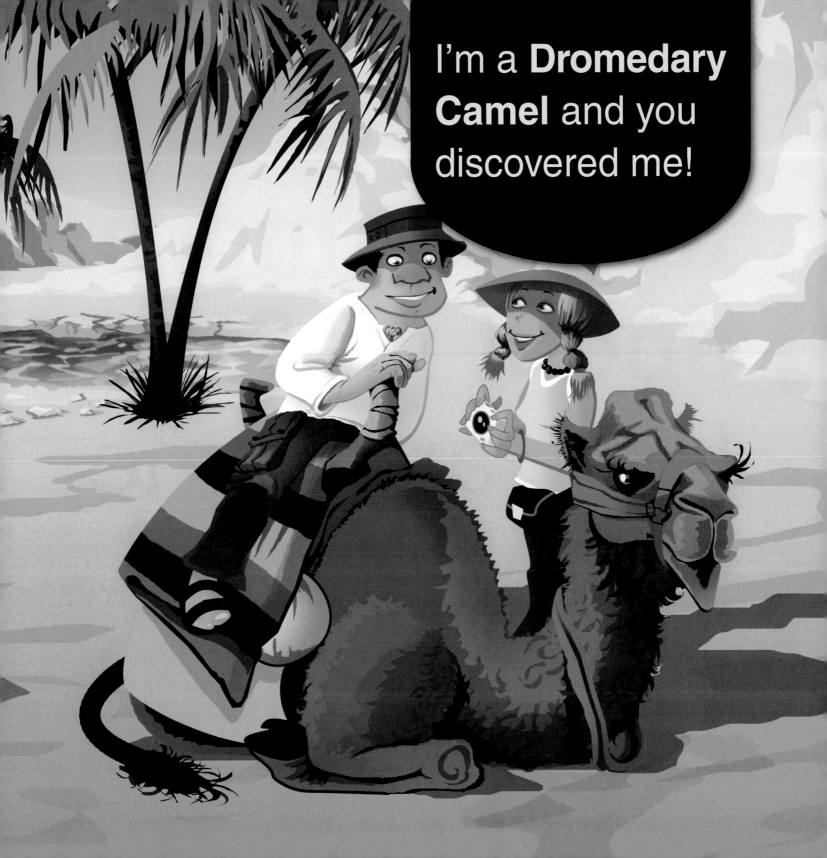

Do you want to know more about me? Here are some Dromedary Camel fun facts.

1. Dromedary camels have one hump.

2. Dromedary camels can live for 30 to 40 years.

3. When thirsty, a dromedary camel can drink up to 32 gallons of water at one time.

4. Dromedary camels usually walk in single file to save energy. This way only the lead camel has to make the trail.

5. Dromedary camels have special eyelids that close and protect their eyes during a sandstorm. Because the eyelid is transparent, they can still see where they are going when it is closed.

6. A dromedary camel can walk for hours at a time with a rider on its back.

7. Dromedary camels are no longer considered wild animals. They are domesticated animals, which means they are taken care of by humans.

Who, What, Where, When, Why, and How

USE THE QUESTIONS who, what, where, when, why, and how to help the child apply knowledge and process the information in the book. Encourage him or her to investigate, inquire, and imagine.

In the Book...

DO YOU KNOW WHO nurses the baby camel for the first year of its life?

DO YOU KNOW WHAT the featured mammal in the book is?

DO YOU KNOW WHERE dromedary camels live?

DO YOU KNOW WHEN a dromedary camel's special eyelid closes?

DO YOU KNOW WHY dromedary camels have a fleshy mound on their backs?

DO YOU KNOW HOW many toes a dromedary camel has on each foot?

In Your Life...

Dromedary camels walk single file to save energy. Think of some situations when you have to walk single file.

CROSS-CURRICULAR EXTENSIONS

Math

There are 18 dromedary camels walking single file across the desert. Halfway through the journey, 6 stop walking. Another 3 stop shortly thereafter. How many of the 18 dromedary camels finish together?

Science

Dromedary camels are herbivores. Research what a herbivore is and what specific vegetation a dromedary camel eats.

Social Studies

What are some differences or similarities between a desert and the area where you live?

Fun Activity

You have uncovered the clues and discovered the dromedary camel. As stated in the Fun Facts, dromedary camels are domesticated animals. They are taken care of by humans.

ASSIGNMENT
Write a story about a domesticated dromedary camel and another domesticated animal that is taken care of by the same person.

IMAGINE
Who takes care of the animals?
What is the other animal?
Where are they kept?
When do they eat?
Why do they need a human to take care of them?
How do they get along?

WRITE
Enjoy the writing process while you take what you have imagined and create your story.

UNCOVER
&DISCOVER

Author

Robert Kanner is part of the writing team for the Uncover & Discover series as well as the Global Adventures and Holiday Happenings series. An extensive career in the film and television business includes work as a film acquisition executive at the Walt Disney Company, a story editor for a children's television series, and an independent family-film producer. He holds a bachelor's degree in psychology from the University of Buffalo and lives in the Hollywood Hills, California, with Tom and Miss Murphy May.

Illustrator

Since graduating from Falmouth School of Art in 1993, **Russ Daff** has enjoyed a varied career. For eight years he worked on numerous projects in the computer games industry, producing titles for Sony PlayStation and PC formats. While designing a wide range of characters and environments for these games, he developed a strong sense of visual impact that he later utilized in his illustration and comic work. Russ now concentrates on his illustration and cartooning full-time. When he is not working, he enjoys painting, writing cartoon stories, and playing bass guitar. He lives in Cambridge, England.